Guide To

The FormTool PRO,
Doxserá,
and
Doxserá DB

By Bill Cutchin

User's & Administrator's Guide To

The**FormTool** PRO,

Dox**será**,

and

Dox**será** DB

Bill Cutchin

Acknowledgments

I would like to acknowledge the cooperation, efforts, and encouragement of Bob Christensen, Scott Campbell, and all the staff at TheFormTool, LLC, without whose programs and help this work would never have been written.

Table of Contents

Introduction

Part 1
User's Guide

Welcome to Document Automation

The Form

The Questionnaire

The Program Tab for End-Users

Large Forms and Error Messages

Doxserá Special Features

Doxserá DB Special Features

Part 2
Administrator's Guide

What to Expect

How To Install the Program

The Program Tab for the Administrator

Templates

Maintenance

Introduction

*Welcome to the Wonderful
World of
Document Automation!*

Document Automation, also sometimes called Document Assembly, allows you to rapidly complete the documents and forms you use on a frequent basis.

Although there are several Document Automation software products available, I have found that the best ones with the greatest value are The**Form**Tool PRO, **Dox**será, or **Dox**será **DB**, all of which are made and sold by TheForm-Tool, LLC (*www.TheFormTool.com*). For convenience, in this book I refer to whichever of these three programs you use as the Program. Accordingly, this book is strictly about how to use those Programs.

This is NOT a book about programming or authoring Forms. This book is for the end-user of the Program, the person who will actually be using the Program on a day-to-day basis to produce "error-free" Documents.

This book is also for the Administrator of the Program, the person who will install the Program and the Templates and be responsible for maintaining everything.

About This Book

This book is divided into two major sections:

- The first, the User's Guide, is for the day-to-day user of the Forms;

- The second, the Administrator's Guide, is for the Administrator, or the person who will install the Program on the computer and who will be responsible for updating the Forms as necessary.

I have written this book to be as non-technical as possible. Nonetheless, there are portions which may be somewhat technical. To aid in understanding, I have included a Glossary at the end to define certain words or phrases which may not be self-explanatory.

Although you may want to read this book from cover-to-cover, it is also designed so you can look at just the parts on which you need an explanation or help. The purpose of the book is to be a reference in your use of the Program and to help you produce your work more efficiently and effectively.

What the Program Does

The Program takes a Document with which you are probably already familiar and allows you to complete the changeable parts of the Document by answering different questions and then clicking one button. The Document is then completed by the Program as an "error free" Microsoft Word Document with all the answers you have given inserted in the proper places. The Program also may

- Change the endings of singular and plural nouns and verbs,
- Perform mathematical functions and/or date functions and enter the correct answer where needed, and
- Automatically add or delete parts of the Document as necessary depending on the various conditions you have entered as Answers.

For more information about the Program, see the section "What the Program Can Do for You" on page 2.

First, a word about terminology.

This User's Guide has a Glossary at the end to assist you in understanding the different terms used in the Program and in this User's Guide. Each of the terms defined in the Glossary begins with an upper-case letter in this User's Guide. So, when you see a term beginning with a capital letter, you can find a definition for it in the Glossary.

You may be using The**Form**Tool PRO, **Dox**será, or **Dox**será **DB**. Regardless which of these Programs you have, this User's Guide will explain what the Program does and how you can use it.

All three Programs share the same basic features. However, **Dox**será and **Dox**será **DB** have extra additional features which they share, and **Dox**será **DB** has additional features which are not in **Dox**será or The**Form**Tool PRO. I have written separate chapters for any special features which are only available in **Dox**será or **Dox**será **DB**. Except for the information in those particular chapters, everything in this User's Guide applies equally to the Program you have.

Also, throughout this User's Guide, again simply for convenience, I will refer to the various documents and forms which are being automated as Forms. The word Document will mean a Form which has been completed and/or a file you save in Word as an ordinary Word Document (which is what you are used to doing).

Because the Program is so versatile, it can and will be used by various and different professions. Those professions may call the people they help clients, customers, patients, or other names. To simplify things, I have called these people Customers throughout this book. Just substitute the term you use in your profession whenever you see the word Customer.

In some places I will tell you which keys on the keyboard to press. I have put any key you should press in bold and italics. If there are a combination of keys you should press, I have indicated that by the name of the first key which you should hold down, followed by the plus (+) sign, followed by the key you should press and release. For example, ***ctrl+tab***

---

will indicate you need to hold down the **ctrl** key while you press the **tab** key.

About Me and Certification

The author of this book is Bill Cutchin. I have been working with Document Automation for several years using different programs. I own DocAssembly Guru, LLC, (*www. DocAssembly.Guru*), a company which operates as a Form Author for its customers. DocAssembly Guru, LLC takes the Documents its customers are already using and converts them into Forms using The**Form**Tool PRO, **Dox**será, or **Dox**será **DB**.

A while ago TheFormTool, LLC (*www.TheFormTool.com*), the company which created and sells the Programs, created a Certification Program for Form Authors (*https://www.TheFormTool.com/certification/*). This Certification Program is an intense training and learning program to produce efficient, knowledgeable, and experienced Form Authors. As a result of entering and completing the Certification Program, Bill Cutchin proudly has earned the title of *Certified Creator: Intelligent Documents*™.

If you have any questions about anything in this book, or any comments or ways to improve the book, please write me at *Bill@DocAssembly.Guru*.

Part 1
User's Guide

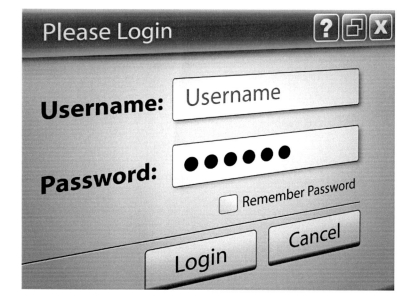

Welcome to Document Automation

If This Is The First Time You Have Ever Used Document Automation, You Are Going To Love It!

You will find it will significantly <u>increase</u> your productivity while significantly <u>reducing</u> your work-load. Studies have shown that using Document Automation improves speed and efficiency from 20% to 70%.

In a nutshell, Document Automation, also sometimes called Document Assembly, allows you to rapidly complete the documents and forms you use on a frequent basis. Each of those Documents and Forms will have assorted items within them which change depending on whom the Document is for or what the situation may be. Those items which change from time to time are known as **Variables**. The remaining items in the Document or Form do not change and are known as **Boilerplate**.

Document Automation asks you to enter the Variables in a Question and Answer format; you merely answer each Question. You then simply click once and the entire Document is completed for you **error free!**

This User's Guide

This User's Guide will explain to you:

- What the Program can do for you;
- The different Forms you will be using;
- How to open and close the Forms properly;
- How to complete the Questionnaire at the end of the Form;
- The distinct Commands in the Program Tab you will be using; and
- Certain advanced items you may or may not use from time-to-time.

What the Program Can Do for You

The purpose of the Program is to take Word Documents you use on a frequent basis and allow you, in the easiest manner possible, to produce them "error free." The Program requires you to enter the unique items (Variables) for the

Form, such as the Customer's name, address, and other such information, just one time, regardless of how many times that information is used in the Form. You do not have to "cut and paste" information each time it is used in the Form.

Also, you can save and reuse the Answers you have entered without having to re-enter them. This is especially helpful if you are preparing different Forms which may use the same, or most of the same, information.

The Forms you will be using are those that have been properly programmed by a Form Author as a Template. **You do not have to worry about programming the Template or how it works.** You will merely Answer the Questions, click a button, and your Form will be automatically completed for you without any typing errors. (Unless, of course, you made a mistake Answering the Questions, but you can easily correct that).

Once you have Answered the Questions, the Program uses your Answers to complete the finished Form with your information inserted in the proper places. You can then save your Answers and use them again in another Form without having to re-enter the same information.

Although it sounds a lot like the "cut and paste" method you are currently using, this is a far superior method of preparing Documents.

- Using the Program, you only have to enter a particular item of information once. Then, even if the Answer is used multiple times throughout the Form, and even in multiple Forms, the Program will insert it correctly for you in each location. So you do not have to find where to "paste" that information within the Form.

- You can save the Answers for one Form and use them in another Form without having to re-enter the Answers again.

- Additionally, you can often give the gender of the individual whose name you enter and, if the Form calls for it, the Program will automatically enter "her" or "his" or "its" (or other appropriate pronoun or word) in the proper places in the Form without you doing anything further.

- If there is a possibility of multiple items being used, such as a list of names, the Program will automatically use the appropriate singular or plural form of both the noun and an associated verb. And you don't have to do anything extra!!

- Another great feature of the Program is that it will automatically perform mathematical and date calculations based on the information you enter, and place the results of those calculations, formatted correctly, in the proper place in the Form.

- And yet another great feature, in a list of great features too long to list here, is that it will take the information you enter and change parts of the Form accordingly.

  - For example, suppose you have a Form which uses one paragraph if the person is married and a different paragraph if that person is a single individual. Depending on the answers you give to certain questions, the Program will include one of those paragraphs and delete the other one, automatically, accurately, and without you having to decide which paragraph to enter and which to leave out.

In summary, you will simply Answer some Questions, click on a button, and your Form will be automatically completed for you, totally error-free, *ready* for you to use as a Word Document!

The Form

The Different Forms You Will Be Using

As you work with the Program you will be using both Forms and Templates. The difference between these two is simple: a Form is what you have been using in Word, except it has been programmed to accept Answers. If you are able to see the extensions on the file names, the extension will be .docx. If you already have a Form saved in a folder with a filename, and you change the Form and then save it, the existing file will be overwritten.

Templates look exactly like Forms, with one major exception. When you open a Template in the proper way, Word does not open the original Template itself, but instead it presents a copy of the Template for you to use (the Form). You will notice that at the top of the screen it will say "Document" and then a number, such as "Document2."

Document2 - Word

Example of a Heading Wehn
Opening A Template

This indicates that you are not typing on the Template itself, but that you have used the Template to open a new Form. This way, you now have the Form you are working on as well as the original Template (which has not been changed). When you save that Form, it will not overwrite the Template. Instead, it will be saved as a new Document file to which you will have to assign it a new filename. The Template will remain unchanged. Thus, you can reuse the Template any number of times and not have to worry that you have over-written it with the changes you made.

Opening the Form

Your Administrator will explain to you exactly which Templates have been programmed and are ready for your use. She/he will further explain to you where, on your computer, these Templates are located.

Opening a Document or Form (Filename.docx)

Documents and Forms in Word have a file name and an extension. The extension, which may or may not show on your computer, will be in the form of **.docx** (usually you will not see the extension, so don't worry about that). This extension indicates to the computer that this file is a Word Document, and it allows you to process the Document or Form as you have always done.

To open a Word Document or Form, you merely click on "Open" as you have normally been doing. You then select the file and either double-click on it or click on "Open."

Opening a Template (Filename.dotx)

The Templates you will be using with your program will have a **.dotx** or **.dotm** extension, which may or may not be shown on your computer. Again, if you are not able to see the extension, that is OK. Your Forms are initially opened when you open a Template.

There are different ways to open a Template to be used by the Program, depending on the version of Word you are using.

- **If you are using Word 2007, you will Click on the Microsoft Office Button in the top left of the Word window and then click on Open from the pop-up menu. In the left window, click on Trusted Templates and select the Template that you wish to open. Click on the Open button. The Template should now be open.**

- **If you are using Word 2010, on the File Tab, click New. Under Available Templates, click My Templates, click the Template that you want, and then click *OK*.**

- **If you are using Word 2013 or Word 2016, click the File Tab. The File screen appears. Choose New from the left side of the File screen. The Featured** part of the New screen appears. It lists Word's own Templates. To look at a list of your Templates, click the Personal (or it may say Shared) heading. Click on a Template to start a new Form using that Template.

In addition to the above methods, you may also open File Explorer, locate your Template, double-click on the name, and it will open properly.

Closing the Form

Closing the form will be practically the same if you opened a previously saved Form or opened a Template. When you are through, you will merely click on the Word Save Command as you have always done and save the Form. If you opened a Template, Word will ask you for a new file-name and directory in which to save the Form.

You will learn in the "The Program Tab for End-Users" on page 29 about Filling and Petrifying a Form, but just remember now that you can save the Form either before or after you have either Filled or Petrified the Form. Word will simply save what you have on your screen, regardless of what you are doing in the Program.

Steps to Assemble a Document

Once you have the Form open as discussed on page 8, you will then

1. Click on the Start Command to move the cursor to the first Answer (see page 31);

2. Answer the Questions (see Chapter "The Ques-

tionnaire" on page 13);

3. Click on Fill (see page 31);

4. If you want to remove the Questionnaire from the finished Document, click on the Petrify Command (see page 35);

5. Print and/or save your Document.

The Questionnaire

Information about the Questionnaire

Location of the Questionnaire

The Questionnaire will always be located at the very end of the Form. The easiest way to go to the first question

Question	Answer
	Doxserá DB [c] 2011-2017 Snapdone, Inc.
Name of Customer	[??]
Address of Customer	[??]

Sample Questionnaire

in the Questionnaire is to click on the Program Tab on the Word Ribbon. Then merely click on the Start Command which is always the first Command on the left-hand side of the Program Tab (see image on next page and page 31).

Start
Command

Clicking on the Start Command will move the cursor to the Answer area of the first Question.

As you Answer a Question, press the **tab** key and the cursor will be moved to the next Answer. If you want to go to a previous Answer, press **shift+tab** and the cursor will be moved to the previous Answer.

You may move the cursor to any Answer you wish at any time. As a general rule, you do not have to Answer the Questions in any particular order. The exception to this rule is when some Answers are "Linked" to previous Answers. Typically you will know this is true if the Question includes wording similar to "Be sure you click Refresh after you enter the last piece of information" or if the Question is in a Grid at the bottom of the Questionnaire. This will occur often in Series Items (See page 19).

Different Types of Answers

There are five different types of Answers you will be using:

- Text
- Drop-down
- Yes/no
- Checklist
- Series

If the Questionnaire has been properly prepared by the Form Author, you will have a clear understanding of what type of Answer is needed for each Question. Typically, if there is any doubt, the Form Author will put a hint in the Question. Even so, there may be times when you are not clear what type of Answer is being requested. In these events, the following information will be very helpful to you.

You should also remember that if you do not know the Answer to a Question, you can leave that Answer blank by not entering any information in the space provided.

Text Answers

Text Answers are the most common type of Answers. You can immediately recognize a Text Answer if the only thing in the Answer column for the Question is a single [??]. When you click on the [??], you are then allowed to enter anything you want. When you have completed the Answer, merely press *tab* or click somewhere else on the Form, such as in another Answer space.

Question	Answer
	Doxserá DB (c) 2011-2017 Snapdone, Inc.
Name of Customer	[??]
Address of Customer	[??]

Example of Text Answers

In some cases, you will see a text answer which has [??][??] in the Answer space. This typically occurs when a name is to be entered. When you enter the name in the first [??] and then press *tab*, a down-arrow will appear beside the second [??].

When you click on the down-arrow you will see a drop-down answer of "he", "she", "it", or "they". This list represents the pronoun you need to select for the name you have given.

Doxserá DB (c) 2011-2017 Snapdone, Inc.		
Question	**Answer**	
Name of Customer	[ ] [??] ▾	
Address of Customer	[??] [??]	
	[he]	
	[she]	
	[it]	
	[they]	

Merely select the correct pronoun which correlates with the name.

Text Answers can be text, numbers, or dates, and you are not limited to the number of characters you may use as an Answer. You may type in only one line, or a complete paragraph, or more.

There may be times you need to enter the information in a Text Answer using a certain Format. For example, in some answers you may need to enter a percentage in the Format of 99.99 and in other answers you may need to enter it as .9999. If you need to enter the information in a certain Format, the Form Author should have provided an example of the Format in the Question.

- As an example, when I author a Form and ask for a date, my question may read, "Enter the date of the document. Format: mm/dd/yyyy."

If there are multiple ways of entering an Answer and there is no example of a Format given, then you can enter the Answer using any method you like. In these cases, the Program will usually be able to interpret the information you entered in the Format you used. If not, when you Fill the Form, you will typically get an error message somewhere in the Filled-in

Form. See page 51 for explanations of Error Messages and how to correct them.

Drop-Down Answers

Drop-down Answers can be recognized because just to the right of the [**??**] in the Answer Column, you will see a small down-arrow. Merely click on the down-arrow and the Answers from which you may select are presented to you. Then click on the Answer of your choice. **<u>You may only select one of the Answers presented.</u>**

In some cases, you will be able to either choose one of the Answers presented, or you may be able to enter your own information.

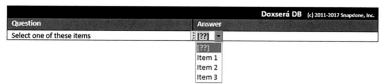

Example of Drop-down Answer

If you do not like the Answers provided, the simple way to verify this is to start typing in the [**??**].

- If nothing happens, you will not be able to enter your own information, and you must select one of the Answers presented.

- If what you are typing appears, it will stay as your Answer to this Question. Of course, you can always change your Answer (See "Changing Answers" on page 25).

Yes/no Answers

Yes/no Answers are almost self-explanatory. Yes/no Answers can be recognized because just to the right of the [**??**] in the Answer Column, you will see a small down-arrow. When you click on the down-arrow you will be given a choice of selecting either "yes" or "no". In some cases you may also see the choice of "n/a" which means not applicable.

Example of Yes-No Answer

Regardless of whether n/a appears, **you may still select only one Answer.**

Checklist Answers

Checklist Answers are easily recognized because a number of different choices for the Answers will appear in the Answer Column, each with an empty box to the left of them.

Example of Checklist Answer

You may select as many of the Answers as you wish. To select an Answer, merely click in the empty box to the left of the Answer. The box will then change to a box with an X in it, indicating you have selected it. If you select something in error, merely click in the box again and the X will disappear.

Series Answers

Series Answers are Answers which can contain more than one piece of information. These can be used in lists, such as a list of names, dates, addresses, etc., which may be an easy way to remember them.

Series Answers may be

- Text Answers,

- Drop-down Answers,

- Yes/no Answers,

- Checklist Answers, or

- The Answers in a Grid (See "Questionnaire vs Grids" on page 20).

	Doxserá DB (c) 2011-2017 Snapdone, Inc.
Question	Answer
What are the name(s) of your customers?	[??] [??] [??]

Example of Series Text Answer

You can recognize a Series Text Answer if there is more than one [??], placed one below the other, in the Answer Column for the Question. If the Answer is a Series Text Answer, enter as many Answers to the Question as needed. If you need to enter more Answers than there are [??]'s, place your cursor in one of the Answer spaces for this Question. Then look in the Series Group of the Program Tab and click on Add (see "Add Command" on page 44). This will add an additional place for another Answer. You may add as many [??]'s as you wish or need.

Series Answers are easy to recognize because there will always be the ability to enter more than one Answer.

Questionnaire vs Grids

The Form Author may put Series Answers in the Questionnaire. While the Form Author may have decided this is the best way to handle a situation, there is another method which is quite frequently used. This is the use of a Grid.

Grids are ALWAYS Serial Answers. Grids will always appear at the bottom of the Questionnaire if they are used. A Grid is similar to a spreadsheet and will appear similar to the following:

This part of the Grid will contain instruction or description of the Grid			
This section will contain a question for the rows directly below it. For example: Name of customer	Address	Birthdate	Is this an employee?
[??]	[??]	[??]	[??]
[??]	[??]	[??]	[??]
			yes
			no

Example of Grid

The information in the first, or left, column must ALWAYS be unique, i.e., you cannot enter the identical information in more than one row in this column. This allows the Program to know specifically which row to use.

The information in all the other columns applies to the Answer in the first column in that row and does not have to be unique. For example, if the first column asks for a name, the second column could ask for the address or other information about the name entered in the first column on that row.

Grids allow you to enter several items of information about related items in a convenient spreadsheet manner.

Unlike the Questionnaire, of which only one can exist in a Form, there may be as many Grids as the Form Author decides to use. The only thing you need to remember is that each Grid is a completely separate set of Answers.

Linking and Linked Answers

Linked Answers are those which are in some way dependent upon another Answer. Linked Answers can appear either in the Questionnaire or in a Grid.

For easy reference, I refer to the major Answer as the Linking Answer, and the dependent Answer as the Linked Answer. You will be able to recognize a Linked Answer because the Answer will either contain [??]:[??], or it will be any column in a Grid other than the left column.

- For example, in one Question (the Linking Answer) you may be asked to enter one or more names of Customers.

- A following Question (the Linked Answer) may ask for the address or birth date of the people you entered in the first Answer.

- These two Questions are Linked because the Answers to the second Question (the Linked Answer) are dependent upon how you answer the first Question (the Linking Answer).

Whenever Linking Answers appear in the Questionnaire there should be a notation in the Question reminding you to "Be sure you click on Refresh after entering the last Answer."

(You will not see this notation in a Grid as the Answers in a Grid do not need to be refreshed.)

Therefore, after entering the last entry for that Linking Answer, you will click on Refresh (see "Refresh Command" on page 36). When you click on the Refresh button, all Linked Answers are refreshed and will show a referral to the Linking Answer.

A simple example of this is a Question asking for names (the Linking Answer) and another Question asking for the address of those people (the Linked Answer).

Linking Answer

Question	Answer
What are the name(s) of your customers? *Be sure to click Refresh after entering the last* *name*	[??] [??] [??]
What is the address of each customer?	[??]: [??]

Linked Answer

Example of Linking and Linked Answers

Therefore, for the Linking Answer you might enter Mary Jones, Tom Smith, and Jerry Black. After you enter the name Jerry Black, you will click on the Refresh button and the Questionnaire will appear as below:

Doxserá DB (c) 2011-2017 Snapdone, Inc.

Question	Answer
What are the name(s) of your customers? *Be sure to click Refresh after entering the last* *name*	Mary Jones Tom Smith Jerry Black
What is the address of each customer?	Mary Jones: [??] Tom Smith: [??] Jerry Black: [??]

You will then enter the address for each person in the appropriate space.

Empty Answers

In Series Answers there may be more spaces to enter Answers than are needed. In this case, simply leave the spaces not needed empty and the Program will ignore them. If you wish to remove an item or a blank space for an item, see "Removing Items" on page 24.

Adding Items

If you need to enter more Answers than there are [??]'s, place your cursor in one of the Answer spaces for this Question. Then look in the Series Group of the Program Tab and click on Add (see "Add Command" on page 44). This will add an additional place for another Answer or an additional row if your cursor is in a Grid. You may add as many [??]'s as you wish or need.

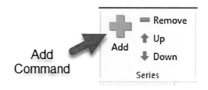

If you have already clicked on the Refresh Command, after you move add, or remove items, you must click on Refresh again.

Moving Items Up or Down

The Program will always use the Linking Answers in the order you entered them. If you wish to change the order of the Answers you have entered, merely place the cursor in the item you want to move and then click on either the Up or Down Command in the Series section of the Program Tab (see "Up Command" on page 45). You may do this multiple times for any item.

If you have already clicked on the Refresh Command, after you move add, move, or remove items, you must click on Refresh again.

Removing Items

If you have entered an Answer and want to delete it, merely select the Answer and press *del* and then *tab*. If you have put an Answer in a Series Answer in a Questionnaire, and you want to remove it, you can either

- Select the Answer and press *del* and then *tab*; OR

- Put the cursor on the Answer to be removed and click on the Remove Command in the Series Group (see "Remove Command" on page 45.)

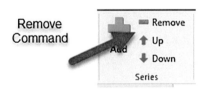

If you like, and this is usually totally unnecessary, you may put the cursor in a [**??**] which has not been answered (you want to leave it blank) and click on the Remove Command in the Series section of the Program Tab (see "Remove Command" on page 45).

If you have already clicked on the Refresh Command, after you move add, move, or remove items, you must click on Refresh again.

Changing Answers

The ability to change Answers is one of the many benefits of the Program. Before you click on the Fill Command, you may change any Answer you wish. Even after you click Fill, if you want to change an Answer, you may do so and then click Fill again. This will reprocess the Answers, including the Answer you changed, and produce the Document with the changed Answer.

You may NOT change the Answer for the Document, however, after you click on the Petrify Command because this Command removes the Questionnaire in producing the Document. But, if you have Saved the Answers, you may reopen the Template, Load the Answers into the Questionnaire, and then change any Answers you wish before you click Fill or Petrify.

For information on Fill, Petrify, and Save/Load Commands, see the "The Program Tab for End-Users" on page 29.

Reuse Answers

When you have completed the Answers in a Questionnaire, you may want to save them so you can use them again. To save the Answers, you must do so BEFORE you click Petrify.

Save/Load
Command

Save/Load
Peek Next
Peek Off

Answers

To save the Answers, click on the Save/Load Command in the Answers Group of the Program Tab. The Saving and Loading Answers dialog box will open.

Full instructions for using the Saving and Loading Answers dialog box are shown in "Save/Load Command" on page 37.

Default Answers

In some situations you may find that an Answer already appears for a Question. This is a Default Answer which the Form Author has provided to help you. If you do not change the Default Answer, it will remain. However, if the Default Answer is not what you want, you may change it to anything you like. You may even delete it if desired.

Because the Default Answer is in the Template, even if you change or delete the Default Answer in your Form, the next time the Template is used, the Default Answer will reappear.

Derived Answers

You may see some Questions which start with the word Derived. These Questions will already have the Answer space completed with some weird looking items.

Your Administrator should have previously removed the Derived Answers so that you do not see them. But, if you do see them you should NEVER enter any information in their Answer space. The purpose of the Derived Answers is to take information you have entered elsewhere and manipulate it in some way.

If you see any Derived Answers, tell your Administrator so they may be properly removed.

The Program Tab for End-Users

Program Tab Appearance

The current Program Tabs for each of the Programs are very similar, but there are some differences.

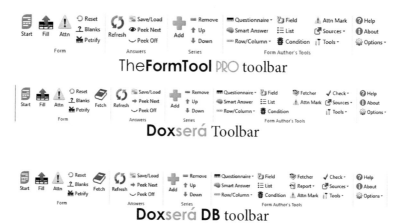

The**FormTool** PRO toolbar

Doxserá Toolbar

Doxserá **DB** toolbar

In the main section of the User's Guide the examples of the Groups in the Program Tab will use those of The**Form**Tool PRO as it contains all of the common Commands. The Chapters on **Dox**será Special Features and **Dox**será **DB** Special Features will use the Tab for those Programs.

How to Use the Program Tab

This section explains the Program Tab and how to use it. To open the Program Tab, merely click on the Program Tab on the Word Ribbon.

Form Group

The Group to the far left of the Program Tab is the Form Group. This contains the **Start**, **Fill**, **Attn**, **Reset**, **Blanks**, and **Petrify** Commands. If you have the **Dox**será Program or the **Dox**será **DB** program, the **Fetch** Command will also appear.

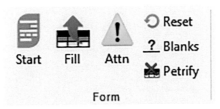

The explanations of the various Commands are given in this Chapter, except the Fetch Command which is only explained in the **Dox**será Special Features and the **Dox**será **DB** Special Features chapters.

Start Command

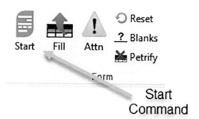

Start Command

After you have opened a Form, if you click on the Start Command the cursor will immediately be moved to the first Answer in the Questionnaire. For another use of the Start Command in **Dox**será and **Dox**será **DB**, see page 57.

Fill Command

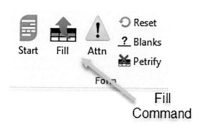

Fill Command

Once you have completed all the Answers you want to enter in the Questionnaire and Grids, click on the Fill Command. Immediately the Program starts "doing its thing." You may see various indications on the screen showing what the Program is doing, but you can ignore those. The Program is now taking the Answers you entered and processing the Form to produce a Document. This process may take a few minutes depending on the complexity of the Form and the age and capabilities of your computer.

When the Program stops running, you will see that the Variables in the Form have all been completed. At this point, you may want to

- Save the Document (which includes the Questionnaire) OR

- Save the Answers OR

- Change one or more Answers and click on the Fill Command again OR

- Petrify the Document.

Also, see "Large Forms and Error Messages" on page 49.

Attention Command

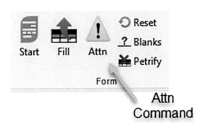

Depending on the Form, the Form Author may have inserted Attention Markers for you. If there are any Attention Markers, you will see a dialog box as soon as the Form has been filled.

These Attention Markers will cause the cursor to go to a specific place in the Form and present you with a dialog box.

The dialog box will have a question or a comment indicating what you should do. If there is more than one Attention Marker in the Form, the Dialog Box will indicate how many more are present.

When you click **OK** on the Dialog Box, the cursor will be placed in the Form in the location to which the Attention Marker is drawing your attention. At this point you may want to enter additional information or otherwise follow the directions in the Dialog Box. When you are through, if the Dialog Box indicated there are more Attention Markers, click on the Attn Command again and you will be taken to the next Attention Marker.

If you click on the Attn Command and there are no more Attention Markers in the Form, the Dialog Box will say, "No Attention Markers" and when you click on **OK** it will no longer appear.

Reset Command

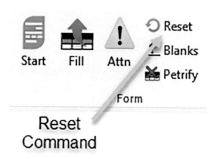

When you click on the Reset Command, all of the Variables in the Form will be reset to their original state. Thus, if you have clicked on the Fill Command and the Variables in the Form have been completed, clicking on the Reset Command will reverse that process and all the Variables will be ready to be Filled again.

Clicking on the Reset Command will not affect the Questionnaire and the Answers you have entered. However, if there are any Derived Answers visible (see "Derived Answers" on page 26), those Answers will be Reset to their original state.

If you accidentally click on the Reset Command, no harm has been done. Simply click on the Fill Command again and the Form will be completed.

Blanks Command

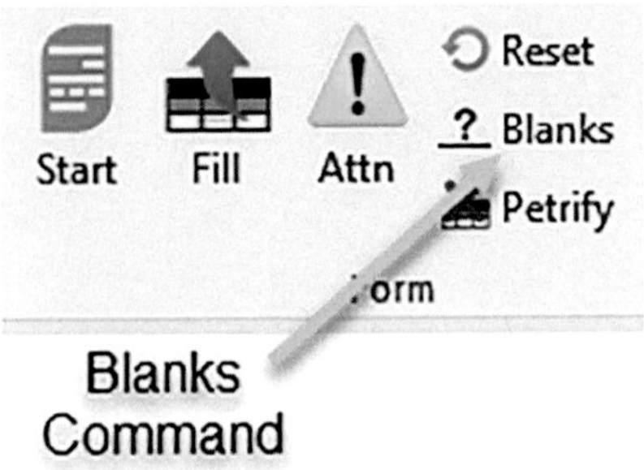

You may want to produce a Document without any Answers being placed in the Form. For example, if you want to produce a Document to give to a Customer or co-worker and you want them to manually fill in the areas which the Program fills in for you, click on the Blanks Command.

Video provides a powerful ________ to help you prove your point. When you click Online Video, you can paste in the embed code for the video you want to add. You can also type a keyword to search online for the ________ that best fits your document.

Example of Blanks

- **Clicking on the Blanks Command does nothing to the Questionnaire, but it will produce a blank line in the Document every place the Form Author had inserted a Field.**

- You can then print the Document and distribute it as you wish without any of your Answers appearing in the Document.

- If you want to distribute the Document with the Blanks but do not want to print the Questionnaire, simply click on the Petrify Command (see "Petrify Command" on page 35) and then click Yes to proceed.

Petrify Command

The Petrify Command is to be used after you click on either the Fill Command or the Blanks Command. The Petrify Command does two things:

- First, it removes the Questionnaire from the Document.

- Second, it permanently sets the Answers in the Document and produces a completed Document for you which you can save, print, or otherwise use as a normal Word Document.

A word of caution — once you click on Yes after clicking on the Petrify Command, the process is NOT reversible. If you did not save the Answers as explained in the "To Save the Answers to a Questionnaire" on page 37, those Answers are now totally gone. If you want to use the Answers, you will have to enter them again. You will not be able to reuse the Answers unless you previously saved them.

Answers Group

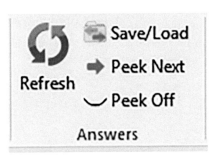

The second Group to the left of the Program Tab is the Answers Group. This contains the **Refresh, Save/Load, Peek Next**, and **Peek Off** Commands.

The explanations of these various Commands are given in this section.

Refresh Command

When you are entering Linking Answers (see section ???) in the Questionnaire (not in a Grid), you will typically see a comment in the Question column for you to "Be sure you click Refresh after entering the last name" or something to that effect.

	Doxserá DB (c) 2011-2017 Snapdone, Inc.
Question	**Answer**
What are the name(s) of your customers?	[??]
Be sure to click Refresh after entering the last	[??]
name	[??]
What is the address of each cu~~stomer?~~	[??]: [??]

Notation to
click Refresh

After you enter the last Answer in a Linking Answer, when you click on the Refresh Command, the Program determines which Answers are Linked to the Linking Answer and it gives the linking information to those Answers. See "Linking and Linked Answers" on page 21 for an example of this.

Save/Load Command

This Command allows you to save the Answers for use later, and it also allows you to Load Answers you have previously saved into the Questionnaire.

To Save the Answers to a Questionnaire

Once you have completed the Answer section of the Questionnaire, or even part of the Answers, you may want to save them to use again either in the Form you are working on or in another Form. To do this, click on the Save/Load Command.

It is important that you remember that the folder names and file names you use in this dialog box WILL NOT change any of the folder names or file names you already have in your computer. Therefore, you may use any names you want without the fear that you are over-writing some other folder or file on your computer.

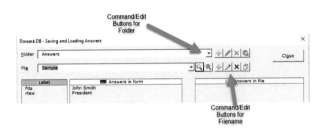

The blank at the top is labeled Folder. Folders have a "parent-child" hierarchy similar to the one you are used to in Word and Windows. "Answers" is the highest level of the hierarchy. You may save all your Answers in the "Answers" folder, or you may add subfolders and sub-subfolders, etc. as you need or want to. To add a subfolder, unless it is to be a subfolder under "Answers," first use the down-arrow to the right of the blank for Folder and select the Folder which you want to be the "parent" subfolder.

Next, with the name of the Folder showing to which you want to add a subfolder, click on the Green Plus sign to the right of the Folder blank. A dialog box will appear which will ask you to enter the name of the new subfolder. Enter the name you want and then click **OK**.

If you want to use another folder which you have already set up, click on the down-arrow to the right of the Folder space. This will show you all the other Folders and subfolders you have set up, and you merely select the one you want to use.

If you want to change the name of a folder, be sure that folder's name appears in the Folder section. Then click on the edit button (the pencil symbol) to the right of that line. Simply enter the name of the folder as you want it and click **OK**. The old name will have disappeared and the new name will appear. Notice that you cannot edit the name of the folder "Answers."

To delete a subfolder, have that subfolder showing in the Folder blank.

- If you want to delete a subfolder and it contains any file(s), you must first delete the files(s) in that subfolder and then delete the subfolder.

- To delete the file(s), click on each one and then click on the Red "X" symbol to the right of the file name. You will then click on Yes to delete that file.

- Then click on the Red "X" key to the right of the subfolder name. You will be asked if you want to remove the subfolder and answer "Yes."

Notice, you cannot delete the folder "Answers."

Once you have selected the folder or subfolder you want to use, either select an existing file within that folder, or add a new file. To add a file, click on the Green Plus symbol to the right of the file blank. Then type in the file name you want to use and click on **OK**.

If you already have numerous file names in that folder, you may click on the search button (the magnifying glass) and find the one you are looking for.

You may also edit the name of a file by clicking on the Edit button (the pencil symbol), change the name, and then click on **OK**.

To Save the Answers

Once you have selected the folder and file to which you want to save the Answers, simply click on the Blue Arrow pointing right (it has the word "save" over it) which is located between the columns. The Answers will be highlighted and a button will appear below the columns with the word "GO" in it.

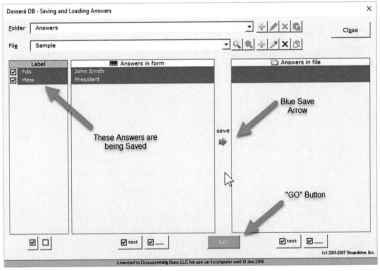

To the left of the Answers will be a column showing which Answers are being saved by showing a check mark in the box to the left of the Answers. If you have saved the Answers previously, only the Answers you have changed will be saved as the others are already saved, and they will be indicated by a check mark in the box to the left of the column of Answers.

- If you want to check all of the Answers, click on the button below the list which has a check mark in it.

- If you want to uncheck all of the Answers, click on the button below the list which does not have a check mark in it.

- If you want to uncheck a particular Answer or if you want to check a particular Answer, click in the box to the left of the Answer.

- If an Answer is highlighted and the box to the left of it is checked, it will be saved to the file.

- If you have deleted an Answer and you want to save the Answers with that Answer being a blank, the box to the left of the Answer will not be checked and you must manually check it to save the blank Answer.

When you are ready to save the Answers, click on the **GO** button and your Answers will be saved. If you are trying to save a blank Answer, you will see a warning box that the Answer you had there will be deleted and a blank will be saved. Answer the warning box according to what you want to do.

To Load Answers

To load Answers you have already saved to the same or a different Form, after you have clicked on the Save/Load Command and selected the folder and file which contains the Answers you want to load into the Questionnaire of the Form you have open, simply click on the Blue Arrow pointing left (it has the word "load" below the arrow). The

Answers will be highlighted and a button will appear below the columns with the word "GO" in it.

Only the Answers which are not already in the Questionnaire will be loaded, and they will be indicated by a check mark in the box to the left of the column of Answers. If you want to check all of the Answers, click on the button below the list which has a check mark in it. If you want to uncheck all of the Answers, click in the button below the list which does not have a check mark in it. If you want to uncheck a particular Answer or if you want to check a particular Answer, click in the box to the left of the Answer. If an Answer is highlighted and the box to the left of it is checked, it will be will be loaded into the Questionnaire.

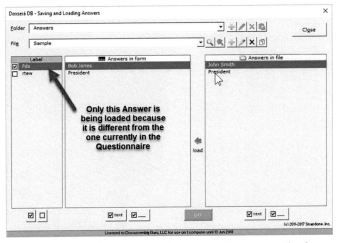

If an Answer is already in the Questionnaire before you Load the Answers, and it is different from the one you are Loading, the existing Answer will be overwritten by the one you are Loading.

When you are ready to load the Answers, click on the **GO** button and your Answers will be loaded into the Questionnaire.

Peek Next Command

From time-to-time, as you complete the Questionnaire, you may want to see where an Answer will actually appear in the Form. To do this, use the Peek Next Command. The Peek Next Command allows you to locate within the Form where a particular Answer will be inserted.

To use this Command, first place your cursor in the Answer column for the particular Answer you want information on. Then click on the Peek Next Command. The screen will then be split, and in the upper screen the cursor will be in the location in the Form where the Answer is used. To find the next location where the Answer is used, just click the Peek Next Command again. You may continue using this process to find all the locations which use that particular Answer.

Peek Off Command

When you are through using the Peek Next Command, click on the Peek Off Command to remove the split screen and return to the Questionnaire. Sometimes, but not often, I have had to click the Peek Off Command twice to remove the split screen.

Series Group

The third Group from the left of the Program Tab is the Series Group. This Group contains the **Add, Remove, Up,** and **Down** Commands.

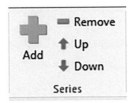

The Commands in this Group are used only for Series Answers (see "Series Answers" on page 19). The Series Answers may be in the Questionnaire; and all of the rows in a Grid are Series Answers. The explanations of the various Commands are given in this section.

Add Command

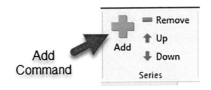

If there are not enough [**??**]'s in a Series Answer in the Questionnaire, or if there are not enough Rows in a Grid for the information you need to add, simply place your cursor in the one of the Answer spaces or in the Row and click on the Add Command. A new [**??**] or Row will be added immediately below the cursor for your use. You can repeat this as often as you need to.

Remove Command

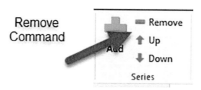

You may want to remove an Answer or a Row you have entered in a Series Text Answer or a Grid. To perform this task, simply place the cursor in the Answer or Row you want to remove and click on the Remove Command.

WARNING: Clicking on the Remove Command MAY BE non-reversible if you change your mind. If you do make a mistake, click the Microsoft Word Undo Command to see if you are able to reverse the Remove Command. You may need to click Undo more than once.

Up Command

If you want to move a Text Serial Answer or a Row up to the position above its current location, merely click on the Up Command. This will move the Text Serial Answer or Row up one location. You can repeat this as often as you need to.

Down Command

If you want to move a Text Serial Answer or a Row down to the position below its current location, merely click on the Down Command. This will move the Text Serial

Answer or Row down one location. You can repeat this as often as you need to.

Form Author's Tools Group

The fourth Group to the left of the Program Tab is the Form Author's Tools Group. This Group contains several Commands, but the only one you need to be concerned with is the **Tools** Command. When you click on the Tools Command, a drop-down list of several additional Commands is presented. The only one of these you will use is the **Clear Answers** Command.

The explanation of the Clear Answers Command is given in this section.

Clear Answers Subcommand

If you have entered Answers in the Questionnaire and/ or Grid and wish to remove ALL of the Answers at one time, you may click on the Clear Answers Command. When you do, a dialog box will appear asking if you are sure you want to clear all of the Answers and reset them to empty values. When you click on Yes, it will delete the Answers you have put in.

Note Well: If you have entered Text Serial Answers in the Questionnaire, you will need to use the Clear Answers Command twice. The first time it will only clear the Linked Answers. When you clear the Answers the second time, it will clear the Linking Answers.

Large Forms and Error Messages

Chapter 5

Items You Might See If You Are Using a Large Form

If your Form is exceptionally large (which usually means over 1,000 fields, lists, and conditions), when you click on the Fill Command you may see a dialog box similar to the one shown on the next page. This screen contains three options, of which you may select any, all, or none.

The first option is **Don't Refresh**. Normally, when you click the Fill Command, the Program attempts to fix any problems with Answers which may exist (see "Refresh Command" on page 36). If you feel at ease with the Answers you have, then click this option and this step of the Program will not be used. This can save you processing time if you have a lot of Answers.

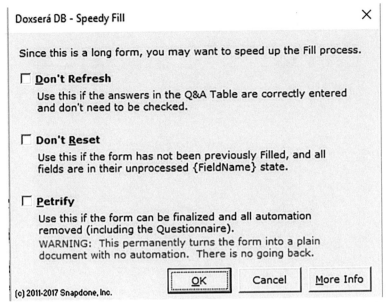

The second option is **Don't Reset**. Normally, when you click the Fill Command, the Program goes through each field, list, and condition and resets them to their original state (see "Reset Command" on page 33). If you have already clicked on the Fill Command or the Blanks Command and did not afterward click on the Refresh Command, then you do not want to check this item. However, if this is the first time you are Filling the Form, you may want to select this option as it may save you some time.

The third option is **Petrify**. If you select Petrify, when you click on *OK* it will Fill the Form and Petrify it in one step (see "Petrify Command" on page 35). While this may save you time, remember that the Petrify Command is not reversible, and it will remove the Questionnaire with all the Answers, so you may want to save your Answers first (see "To Save the Answers to a Questionnaire" on page 37). Therefore, use this option with care.

Error Messages and How To Correct Them

You should never see any Error Messages using the Program. There are some errors, however, which you may make in answering the Questions and which may generate some Error Messages. If an Error Message should appear, see if you can detect the problem and fix it. If you cannot, contact the Administrator.

Here are some typical Error Messages you may see and common ways to fix the error.

ERROR - DATE FORMAT - This Error Message indicates that you put something in an Answer which calls for a date in a format the Program is not able to translate into a date. This usually happens when you have made a typo error.

ERROR - MISSING NUMBER - This Error Message will appear if an Answer which was to be translated by the Program into a number is not in a numeric format. Again, this usually is just a typo which can be easily fixed by you.

To troubleshoot the problem, merely place the cursor on the Error Message in the Form. Then click on the Reset Command in the Program Tab. When the Form has been reset, you will then see the label name of the Variable which has caused the problem. If this name is enough for you to determine which Answer has caused the problem, simply go to that Answer and correct it.

If seeing the label name does not help you decide which Answer is causing the problem, ask the Administrator to show the Labels in the Questionnaire, find that Label, and then correct the Answer.

After you have corrected the Answer causing an Error Message, click again on the Fill Command and the form will be properly filled without the Error Message.

Doxserá Special Features

Special Features for Doxserá

All of the information given previously in this book applies to **Dox**será. This section contains information about features which **Dox**será has but are not available in The**Form**Tool PRO.

There are two features **Dox**será has which The**Form**Tool PRO does not have. These features are the ability to use **Folios** and the ability to use **Form Sets**. The use of both of these features are explained in this chapter.

Folios

Folios store a number of different types of files. Folios are originally set up by the Form Author and can contain a library of text clauses or paragraphs, graphics, footnotes, and other non-text features. You do not need to be concerned with the contents of any Folios.

Fetch Command

In some Forms the Folio information is automatically added due to the programming which the Form Author has done.

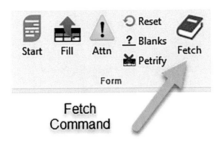

Fetch Command

In other (or perhaps even the same) Forms, you will be asked a Question which you are to Answer using the **Fetch** Command. The Fetch Command is located in the Form Group of the Program Tab on the Word Ribbon.

You will know when to use the Fetch Command because when you put the cursor in the Answer space, a note will pop-up saying, "use Fetch to choose." When you see this pop-up, DO NOT enter an Answer. Instead, merely click on the Fetch Command. At that time you will be given a choice of which Answer(s) to use.

The Fetch Command may use either Drop-down Answers (see "Drop-Down Answers" on page 17) or Checklist Answers (see "Checklist Answers" on page 18). You will be able to recognize the difference immediately.

- For Drop-down Answers, a small circle appears to the left of each Answer. When you click on one of these, the circle is filled to indicate you have chosen it. If you decide to change the Answer, when you click in the circle by another Answer, that circle is filled in and the circle beside your previous choice is now empty. Thus, **for Drop-down Answers you can only select one item**.

- For Checklist Answers, a small square appears to the left of each Answer. When you click on one of these, the square is filled. If you want another Answer, that square is also filled. **You may select as many of these Answers as you wish**. If you select an Answer and then decide you do not want to use it, merely click in the square again and if will now be empty.

When you have selected your Fetch Answer(s), continue answering the other Questions, if any. When you click on the Fill Command, the Form will be filled using the Answers you selected.

Form Sets

In some situations there may be several Forms you want to use which are all needed at the same time. For example, in a real estate transaction, you may need to print a Customer letter, a HUD statement (a form required by the US government), a deed, and a receipt. Each of these Forms may exist separately on your computer.

One way to handle this situation is to individually open each Template, complete the Questionnaire by loading previously saved Answers and/or Answering the Questions individually, Fill the Form, Save the Answer file, and then Petrify (see the "The Program Tab for End-Users" on page 29) and print/save the Document. Then you will repeat the procedure with the next Template, until you have completed them all.

The better way is to use a **Form Set**. A Form Set is a way to organize multiple Forms into a collection (set) of Forms. When you open the Form Set, you will be able to select any or all of the Forms within that group. The Program will then compare all the Questionnaires from the selected Forms and combine the Questionnaires into <u>one</u> Questionnaire so that each necessary Question is only asked once.

You will then Answer the Questions and click the Fill Command. When you click the Fill Command, ALL of the selected Forms will be completed for you at one time. Thus, you do not have to Fill each Form.

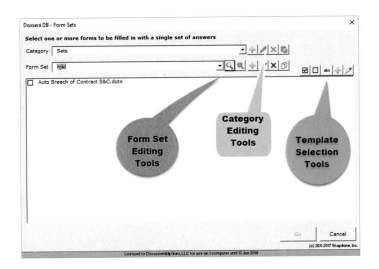

How to Use Form Sets

A Form Set will create multiple Forms for you simultaneously. When Filled, the Documents will remain as individual Documents and will **_not_** be combined into one large Document.

In using Form Sets, you will go through three distinct steps:

1. **Selecting the Forms to use;**
2. **Answering the Questions; and**
3. **Filling in the Forms.**

Selecting the Forms to Use

To begin, open Word and be sure there are no Templates open. This means you will have either a blank Document or a blank screen. Then click on the Start Command (see "Start Command" on page 31). This will open the Form Sets screen.

Select the Category you want to use by clicking on the down arrow to the right of the blank space for Category. Then select the Form Set within that Category which you want to use by clicking on the down arrow to the right of the blank space for Form Set. If you have a lot of Form Sets saved, you can click on the magnifying glass (the search symbol) to find the one you want quickly.

Editing or Adding A New Category and/or Form Set

Category - Add or Edit

Categories are similar to Folders in which you keep related Form Sets. Categories have a "parent-child" hierarchy similar to the one you are used to in Word and Windows. "Sets" is the highest level of the hierarchy. You may add subcategories and sub-subcategories, etc., as you need to.

To add a subcategory (unless it is to be a subcategory under "Sets") first use the down-arrow to the right of the blank for

Category and select the Category which you want to be the "parent" subcategory.

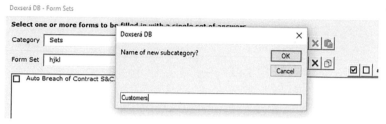

Next, click on the Green Plus sign to the right of the Category blank. A dialog box will appear which will ask you to enter the name of the new subcategory. Enter the name you want and then click **OK**.

To edit (change the name of) a subcategory, have that subcategory showing in the Category blank and click on the Edit button (pencil symbol) to the right of the subcategory name. Then change it as you wish and click **OK**. Notice that you cannot edit the Category name "Sets."

If you want to delete a subcategory and it contains any Form Set(s), you must first delete the Form Set(s) in that subcategory and then delete the subcategory. To delete a subcategory, have that subcategory showing in the Category blank. Then click on the Red "X" button to the right of the subcategory name. You will be asked if you want to remove the subcategory and answer "Yes." Notice, you cannot delete the Category "Sets."

Form Set - Add or Edit

If you have not yet created a Form Set, or if you want to create another Form Set, first select the Category or subcategory in which you want to save the Form Set. Then click on the Green Plus symbol to the right of the blank space for

Form Set. Enter the name for the Form Set (be sure you use something relevant and easy to remember) and click **OK**.

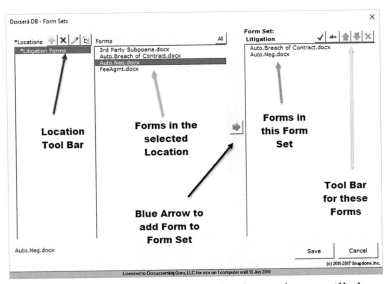

You will then see a dialog box. The first column will show various locations if you have used any locations previously. (The name of each location will be preceded by an asterisk (*), which you can ignore.) A location should be a Folder which contains ONLY Templates, but this is not required. To create a new location, click on the Green Plus symbol in the upper left hand corner of the dialog box which will open a warning. Read the warning and click **OK**. You will then select the Folder you want to use. When you click on **OK** you will be given a choice of using the Folder name or using another name for the location. If you use another name, the name of the Folder will not be changed on your computer. This name will only be used as a location name for the Form Set commands.

When you click on the name of a location, the File names in that Folder will appear in the middle section of the dialog box. Individually select the Templates you want to add to the Form Set and click on the Blue Arrow to the right of the "Forms" column for each one you select. If the Folder contains files other than Templates, BE SURE YOU ONLY ADD TEMPLATES.

The Template you have selected will now appear in the column on the right side of the dialog box. Repeat until you have entered all the Templates you want into the Form Set. Notice that you can "mix and match" Templates from any of the locations to be included in this Form Set. Thus, once you have added the Templates from one location, simply select another location and add Templates from that location.

Once you have selected the Templates you want in the Form Set, you may arrange them alphabetically by clicking on the "abc" button, or you may move the Templates up or down using the up and down arrows. The Forms will be produced in the same order as this list of Templates.

If you change your mind and do not want a selected Template in this Form Set, simply highlight that Template and click on the Red "X" button. You can add it back to the list if you wish by selecting it again in the middle column and clicking on the Blue Arrow to the right of the "Forms" column.

Once you have the forms you want in the Form Set and you have them in the order you want, click on "save".

Editing or Deleting a Form Set

If you want to change the name of the Form Set, select that Form Set and click on the Edit button (pencil symbol), type in the name you want, and click **OK**.

To delete a Form Set, select the name of the Form Set and click on the Red "X" and click on Yes in the dialog box that appears.

You may want to copy a Form Set and perhaps put it in another Category. If you want to copy a Form Set, click on the copy button (the one on the far right of the Form Set blank space). This will show that it has been placed on your clipboard. Change the Category if you like. To add it to your list of Form Sets, click on the paste button (the one on the far right of the Category blank space). The copy will now appear in the list of Form Sets in the Category you have chosen, and you can edit the name if you wish.

If you want to change the Forms you have in a Form Set, click on the Edit button (pencil symbol) which is just above the large box containing the names of the Forms in the Form Set. This will take you back to the screen where you first added Forms to the Form Set.

Once you have selected the Form Set you want to use, a list of all the Templates in the Form Set will show at the bottom of the dialog box.

- You may add a Template temporarily to the list of Templates by clicking on the Green Plus symbol.

- If you wish to add a Template permanently or otherwise permanently change the list, click on the Edit button (pencil symbol).

- You may also change the order of the Templates into alphabetical order by clicking on the "abc" button. Clicking the "abc" button again will put the Templates in their original order.

- If you want to otherwise change the order of the Forms, click on the Edit button (pencil symbol) and use the up and down arrows as explained previously.

You will now select the Templates you want to use. If you click on the box in the third row of symbols (the Template Selection Tools) with the check mark in it, all of the Templates on the screen will be selected. If you click on the empty box, all Templates you had selected will be cleared. You may also click on the box beside the name of a Template to select it or, if it is already checked, to unselect it.

Once you have selected the Templates you want, click on the "Go" button. The Program will now create a single Questionnaire to be used for the Templates you selected.

Answering the Questions

Answer the Questions as you normally would. If you like, you may Load Answers you have previously Saved, and you may also Save the Answers to this Questionnaire (see "To Save the Answers to a Questionnaire" on page 37).

Filling in the Forms

When you have completed the Answers, click on the Fill Command. You will then see a dialog box concerning "Petrification" and "Saving".

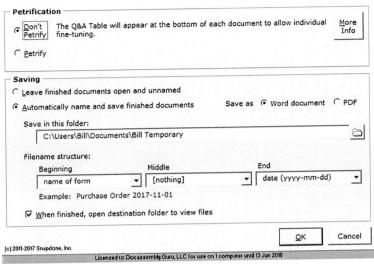

The "Petrification" section allows you to choose to either "Don't Petrify" the Form after it is competed, or to Petrify it.

If you select "Don't Petrify," you will be able to change the Answers and Fill the Forms again. If you select Petrify (see "Petrify Command" on page 35), after Filling the Forms, the Program will automatically delete the Questionnaire and prepare the Forms as Word Documents.

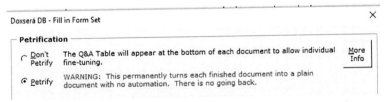

If you select Petrify, and click on **OK**, the Petrify procedure is permanent and you cannot reverse it. (Although, of course, you can use the Form Set again to create the Forms again. This is especially easy if you Saved the Answers.)

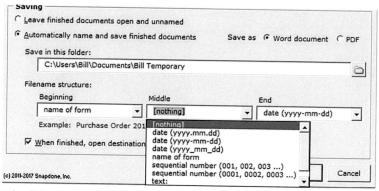

The "Saving" section concerns how you may want to save the Forms, and not how you want to Save the Answers.

- The first choice you have is to leave all the resulting Forms or Documents open, unnamed, and not saved in any Folder. You will then have to save each of the Forms or Documents individually.

- The second choice is to have the Program automatically name and save the Documents in a Folder you select. If you choose this option, you then need to indicate if you want the Documents saved as Word Documents or as PDF files.

- Next, you need to select the Folder in which you want the Documents saved.

- Finally, you will select how you want the filename to read.

  - You are given three sections of the filename you may use: Beginning, Middle, and End.

  - When you click on the down arrow to the right of each selection, you will see the various choices you may select from, including nothing.

  - If you select text, you will be asked to fill in the text you want in the filenames.

- As you complete the three sections of the filename, you will be shown an example below the three selection areas of how the filename will look.

- You may also select to open the destination folder when the Program has completed to allow you to view the files.

When you have finished with this dialog box, click **OK** and your instructions in this dialog box will be performed by the Program.

Doxserá DB
Special Features

Special Features for **Doxserá DB**

All of the information given previously in this book, including the special features for **Doxserá**, applies to **Doxserá DB**. This section contains information about features which **Doxserá DB** has but are not available in either The**Form**Tool PRO or **Doxserá**.

The "**DB**" in **Doxserá DB** stands for Data Base. This allows you to use the information in a data base as well as the information you enter in the Questionnaire. The database does NOT need to be open when you complete the Questionnaire and Fill the Form, so you do not need to worry about the operations of the database.

Fetch Command

One of the Questions, and sometimes the only Question, in the Questionnaire will ask you to select which item in the data base you want to use. When you click in the Answer column for this Question, you will know to use the Fetch Command because a note will pop-up saying, "use Fetch to choose." When you see this pop-up, DO NOT enter an Answer. Instead, merely click on the Fetch Command.

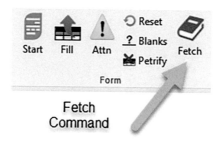

Fetch
Command

The Fetch Command is located in the Form Group of the Program Tab on the Word Ribbon. When you click on the Fetch Command, a dialog box will appear. This dialog box contains two Tabs, "Normal" and "MultiDoc". The "Normal" Tab will allow you to create one Document, while the "Multi-Doc" Tab will allow you to create many Documents.

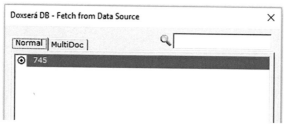

If you click on the "Normal" Tab, you will be presented with a list of items in the database. Select the item you want to use for this Form.

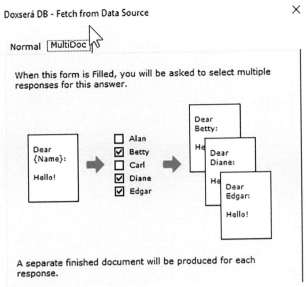

If you click on the "MultiDoc" Tab, you will see an information box telling you that you will select the Answers when
you click the Fill Command. Just click **OK** to have the information box removed.

When you have selected your Fetch Answers, continue
answering the other Questions, if any. When you click on
the Fill Command, if you clicked on the "Normal" Tab, the
Form will be filled using the Answers you selected.

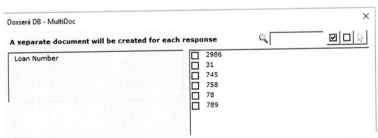

If you clicked on the "MultiDoc" Tab you will see a dialog
box asking you to select as many of the selections for which
you want separate documents. You may select one or more
of the Answers given. If there are many choices, you can

enter information in the search box and click on the search (magnifying glass) icon.

- If you want to select all of the Answers, click on the box which contains the check mark.

- If you want to unselect all the Answers you have selected, click on the empty box.

- You can click on the arrow to change the selection mode. If you do that,

  - You can then click to select a single Answer, *ctrl+click* to select additional Answers, or *shift+click* to select a range of Answers.

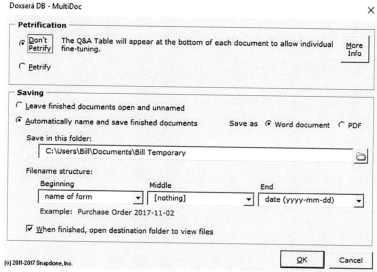

When you have completed the Answers, click on the Fill Command. You will then see a dialog box concerning "Petrification" and "Saving".

The "Petrification" section allows you to choose to either "Don't Petrify" the Form after it is completed, or to Petrify it.

If you select "Don't Petrify," you will be able to change the Answers and Fill the Forms again. If you select Petrify (see

"Petrify Command" on page 35), after Filling the Forms, the Program will automatically delete the Questionnaire and prepare the Forms as Word Documents. If you select Petrify, and click on **OK**, the Petrify procedure is permanent and you cannot reverse it. (Although, of course, you can use the Form Set again to create the Forms again. This is especially easy if you Saved the Answers.)

The "Saving" section concerns how you may want to save the Forms, and not how you want to Save the Answers.

- The first choice you have is to leave all the resulting Forms or Documents open, unnamed, and not saved in any Folder. You will then have to save each of the Forms or Documents individually.

- The second choice is to have the Program automatically name and save the Documents in a Folder you select. If you choose this option, you then need to indicate if you want the Documents saved as Word Documents or as PDF files.

- Next, you need to select the Folder in which you want the Documents saved.

- Finally, you will select how you want the filename to read.

  - You are given three sections of the filename you may use: Beginning, Middle, and End.

  - When you click on the down arrow to the right of each selection, you will see the various choices you may select from, including nothing.

  - If you select text, you will be asked to fill in the text you want in the filenames.

  - As you complete the three sections of the filename, you will be shown an example below the three selection areas of how the filename will look.

- You may also select to open the destination folder when the Program has completed to allow you to view the files.

When you have finished with this dialog box, click **OK** and your instructions in this dialog box will be performed by the Program.

Part 2 Administrator's Guide

What to Expect

Chapter 8

Tasks as Administrator

As Administrator, you have the responsibilities of installing the Program, changing the file locations, and several other duties, including helping the end-users of the Program.

This part of the book will be of tremendous help to you in performing these duties. I also HIGHLY RECOMMEND you print and review the pertinent parts of the Expert Guide you received when you downloaded the program. If for any reason you do not have access to the Expert Guide, you can download it for free at ***https://service.TheFormTool.com/hc/en-us/sections/202697906-Guides-and-Manuals***.

If you should have questions about any of this, please feel free to contact me at *Bill@DocAssembly.Guru*.

Definitions

I have provided a Glossary at the end of the book to explain any of the terms which begin with an uppercase letter. If the Glossary does not adequately explain a term for you, please refer to the Expert Guide you received from TheFormTool, LLC when you purchased the Program, or please feel free to contact me at *Bill@DocAssembly.Guru*.

Steps to take

The steps you will ordinarily initially take are

1. Install the Program (see "How To Install the Program" on page 81).

2. Install the Templates you received from the Form Author (see "Templates" on page 107).

3. Install any Master Lists (see "How to Install a Master List" on page 88) and/or Folios (see "Folios Subcommand" on page 91) you received from the Form Author.

4. Remove the labels from the Questionnaire (see "Show/Hide" on page 86).

5. Explain to the end-user(s) how to open the Forms (see "Opening the Form" on page 8) and where the Documents should be saved.

6. Maintain the Program as needed (see the "Maintenance" on page 109).

Versions of Word

The Programs work with any version of Microsoft Word from version 2007 through the current version. Each of the versions have different methods to open Templates, so please refer to "Opening a Template (Filename.dotx)" on page 9 to see the method for your version of Word.

How To Install the Program

Installing the Program

Before you install the Program, you must have Microsoft Word installed on the computer on which you are going to install the Program. If you have not already, download the Program from *www.TheFormTool.com*. It will download as a .zip file, so you must extract the files. I suggest you use the default folder when extracting the files, but you can change it if you like. The reason I use the default folder is that the same name will appear each time you download and extract an update to the Program.

When the files have been extracted, open the Readme.txt file and follow those instructions. Notice that you must NOT have Word open when you install the Program. The installation program will open Word for you.

If you have any questions on installing the Program, refer to the section in the Expert Guide you received with the Program concerning Installing the Program. This will guide you through the installation step-by-step as well as helping you solve any problems you may have with the installation. Again, you may contact me at Bill@DocAssembly.Guru.

Who can use the program

The Programs are licensed to computers, and not to people. Therefore, even if you have ten users, if the Program is only installed on one computer, you only need one license. All of the users can use the Program on that computer.

If you have the Program installed on more than one computer, again any number of users will be allowed to work on the Program on each computer.

Different machines

From the website of www.TheFormTool.com:

"If you only use one computer at a time AND they are not connected on the same LAN, WAN or virtual network, then a single license will work for you. This allows the use of TFT [the Program] on an office machine, but also to work on documents on a home machine or laptop from time to time.

"If the usage is more intense and you want to share templates, documents, or data transparently among machines or between users, then you'll want two licenses.

"Note: Remember that DropBox, Box and similar systems are virtual networks. If you share data between two or more computers through one of them or a similar service, you'll want multiple licenses."

Network

From the website of www.TheFormTool.com:

"TheFormTool and Doxserá can do network installs in a two-step process:

"1. Install normally on one computer, add Registration Name and License Code [see "License Code" on page 101], and set Path [see "Path" on page 104] to desired shared server location. After you've successfully installed the program on one machine, then

"2. Copy these two files from the first computer and distribute them to the same locations on other users' computers. Assuming default profile locations and default Word startup folder locations, those two files are located at:

"a.   C:\Users\[username]\AppData\Roaming\TheFormTool\TheFormTool.ini

"b.   C:\Users\[username]\AppData\Roaming\Microsoft\Word\STARTUP\TheFormTool.dotm"

The Program Tab for the Administrator

The Program Tab

The Program Tab is automatically installed in the Word Ribbon when you install the Program. The Program Tab and the Commands in the Tab are explained in the "The Program Tab for End-Users" on page 29. However, there are some additional Commands you need to know how to use. Those Commands are explained in this Chapter.

Form Author's Tools Group

The Form Author's Tools Group contains the Command buttons you need to be aware of if. They are the **Row/Column** Command, the **Tools** Command, and the **Sources** Command.

Row/Column Command

When you click on the Row/Column Command a menu appears which contains various subcommands. All but one of these subcommands are used exclusively by the Form Author. The one subcommand you need to be aware of is the **Show/Hide** subcommand.

Show/Hide

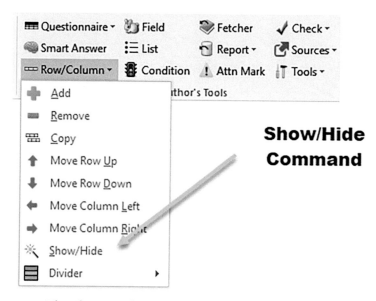

The Show/Hide subcommand is used as a toggle switch to show or hide the **Label** column in the Questionnaire and the labels in any Grids present. When you first install the Template, the Questionnaire will show three columns titled Label, Question, and Answer. A Grid will show the labels as the top row. The items in the Label column and the label row are the names of the variables used by the Form Author, and will typically be irrelevant to you. If the Label column and the label row remain showing, it will typically confuse the end-user as well.

To remove the Label column and the label row of all Grids, merely click on the Show/Hide subcommand. The Program will then remove the Label column in the Questionnaire as well as the label row in any Grids which may be in your Template. Also, it will hide any Derived Answers (see "Derived Answers" on page 26) to further reduce any confusion on the part of the end-user.

If you should decide you want to view the Label column, the Label row in a Grid, and/or the Derived Answers, merely click on the Show/Hide subcommand again.

Sources Command

When you click on the Sources Command a menu appears which contains various subcommands, depending on the Program you are using. If you are using The Form-Tool PRO, **Master Lists** and **Wrapper** will appear. If you are using **Dox**será or **Dox**será **DB**, **Folios** will also appear. Finally, if you are using **Dox**será **DB**, **Data** will also appear. You will not need to use the Wrapper subcommand, but the others are explained here.

Master Lists Subcommand

A Master List is a table of information which can be used in a Template. Master Lists are originally created by the

Form Author. The easiest way to think of a Master List is as a Word table, with rows and columns. A Master List may contain as many rows and columns as are needed.

Name	Description	Price
ABC	Item # 1	4.00
DEF	Item # 2	5.00
GHI	Item # 3	6.00

Example of a Master List

The example shown above has used columns for Name, Description, and Price. This Master List contains a table (or spreadsheet, if you prefer that word) with each row containing a column for the name as well as columns for each of the remaining items of information.

When a Master List is used in a Form, the Questionnaire will only require the user to select which of the rows is to be used, such as selecting the name of someone in the list. When that selection has been made, all of the information about that person which is on the row with the name can be used in the Form without the user having to select it again.

How to Install a Master List

The Form Author will give you any Master Lists when you received the Templates. Each Master List will be a normal Word Document.

To install the Master List in the Program, open the Document as you would a normal Word Document. Then, instead of saving it, click on the Sources Command and then on the Master Lists subcommand as shown on the previous page.

You will then be presented with a dialog box giving you three choices: **Save and Close**, **Continue Editing**, and **Cancel Changes**. Click on Save and Close.

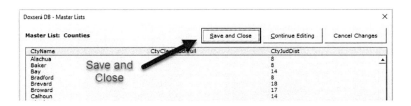

The Master List is now installed and ready for use. If you have more than one Master List, repeat this process for each one.

How to Make Changes In a Master List

Although the Master List will be created by the Form Author, you can make such changes in the Master List as are needed to reflect changing situations. For example, employees will come and go, and their information will need to be added or deleted.

Fortunately making such changes is extremely easy. To make the changes, it does not matter if you have a Form open or not.

- The first thing you will do is click on the Sources Command.

- Then you will select Master Lists.

- A dialog box opens and you will click on the down arrow to the right of blank for Master List. A drop-down list of all the Master Lists you have on the computer will appear.

- You then click on the name of the one you want to change.

- You will then click on the Edit button.

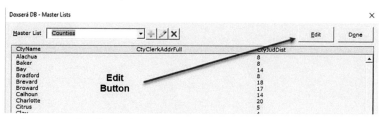

When you do this, the Master List appears in a Word Document as a table. At that point you may delete rows, add rows, or change any information within a cell in the same way you always do with Word tables.

Once you have made the change(s) you want, simply click on the Sources Command and then on Master Lists again (these instructions are on the top of the Master List in case you should forget them.) DO NOT save this as a regular Document if you want the changes to take effect in the Master List.

You will then be presented with a dialog box giving you three choices: **Save and Close**, **Continue Editing**, and **Cancel Changes**.

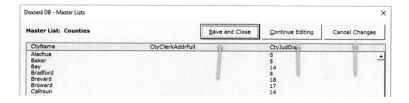

- If you click on Save and Close, the changes you made will be saved and the Master List will close.

- If you click on Continue Editing, the Word table will reopen and you can make more changes if you like. To save it, you will again click on the Sources Command and then on Master Lists.

- If you click on Cancel Changes, the Master List will close but the changes you made will not be saved. An information box will appear to be sure you want to cancel the changes.

Folios Subcommand

The Folios subcommand will appear in both **Dox**será and **Dox**será **DB**. The Form Author will give you any Folios when you received the Templates. Each Folio will be a normal Word Document.

To install the Folio in the Program, open the Document given to you by the Form Author as you would a normal Word Document. Then, instead of saving it, click on the Sources Command and then on the Folios subcommand.

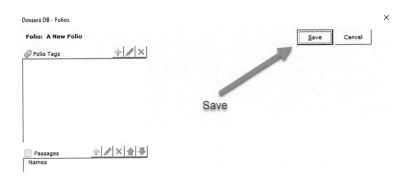

A dialog box will then open. Simply click on the Save button. The Folio is now installed and ready for use. If you have more than one Folio, repeat this process.

Data Subcommand

The Data subcommand is used to let the Program know which databases are to be used and how to use them. Because this process may be different for each of the Templates and/ or databases, you will need to have the Form Author instruct you on the used of the Data subcommand.

Tools Command

The only subcommand in the Tools Command which was not discussed in "Form Author's Tools Group" on page 46 and of which you need to be aware is the **Prepare to Share** subcommand.

Prepare to Share

If you want someone to complete the Questionnaire but that person does not have access to the Program, you can Share the Questionnaire and then use it with a Template. Examples of this sharing might occur

- When someone is out of the office but still has access to a computer;

- When you want to email the Questionnaire to a Customer but do not want them to see the Template, or

- For many other reasons. All the person completing the Questionnaire must have is Microsoft Word version 2007 or newer.

To share the Questionnaire on a Template, you need to open the Template. Then click on the Tools Command and on the Prepare to Share subcommand.

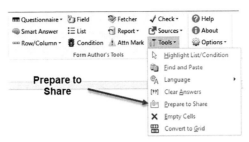

The screen that appears presents several buttons one at a time. You will click on each button in order as you go through this process.

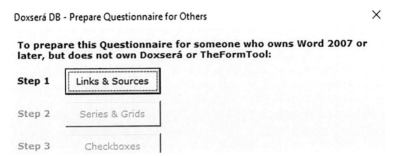

Step 1 is **Links and Sources**. This looks at any Linking and Linked Answers (see "Linking and Linked Answers" on page 21). If those Answers are in the Questionnaire, it may require you to convert them from the Questionnaire into a Grid. If you are uncomfortable doing this, or if you have any problems at all with this, discuss it with the Form Author.

If you are comfortable doing this, place your cursor in the Answer space for the Linking Answer. Then click on the Tools Command and then on the Convert to Grid subcommand. When you are through with this, click again on the Prepare to Share subcommand.

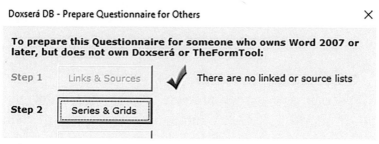

When Step 1 is completed, Step 2, **Series & Grids** is highlighted. When you click on this button, if you have any Series Answers or Grids, you are prompted to be sure you have enough Answers or Rows for the person completing the Questionnaire to enter the information needed. If there are not enough Answers or Rows, click on the Cancel button, add the necessary Answers or Rows (see "Add Command" on page 44), and then click again on the Prepare to Share subcommand.

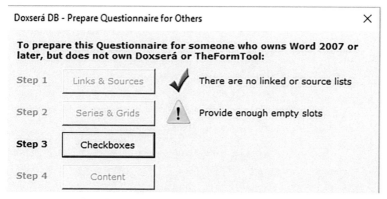

In Step 3, **Checkboxes**, the Program will insure that if you have any checkboxes as Answers (see "Checklist Answers" on page 18), they will be converted to be compatible with Word 2007.

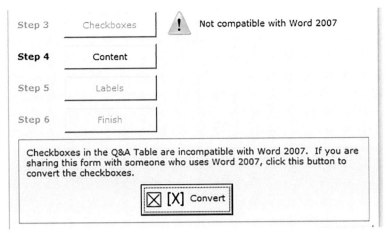

If the Program finds they are not compatible, you can click on the button which appears in the box at the bottom and it will convert them for compatibility with Word 2007.

If you want to share ONLY the Questionnaire and Grids and not the content of the Template, when you click on Step 4 - **Content**, you will see a button in the lower part of the box that says **Remove Content**.

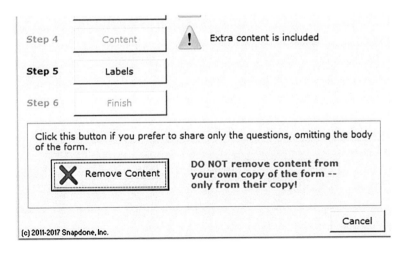

Since you opened a Template for this procedure, when you remove the content it will not be removed from the Template.

However, if you opened a Form as a Word Document, and not as a Template, it will remove the content from that Document.

The Step 5 - **Labels** button allows you to hide the labels in the Questionnaire and/or Grid(s) (see "Show/Hide" on page 86). Just click on the Hide button in the lower part of the box.

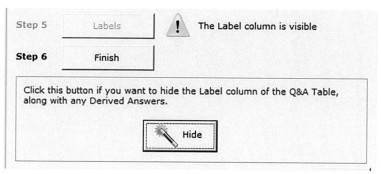

Step 6 - **Finish** completes the process and allows you to share the Questionnaire. At this point you will want to save the Questionnaire so you can use it to share with others.

Now you just have to send by email or other method the Questionnaire to the person who is to complete it. They will open it in their Word program, complete the Answers, and then save it and send it back to you.

When you receive the Questionnaire back, open it as a Word Document. Then click on the Save/Load Command (see "Save/Load Command" on page 37) in the Answers Group and save the Answers. You will then close the Questionnaire as you have finished with it.

Finally, you will open the Template and then load the Answers (see "Save/Load Command" on page 37). You can then change the Answers, or Fill the Form (see "Fill Command" on page 31).

The Unnamed Group to the Right of the Form Author's Tools Group

Help

When you click on the Help Command, a window will open in your Internet browser to the help page on the Program's website. You can then search for the information you need.

About

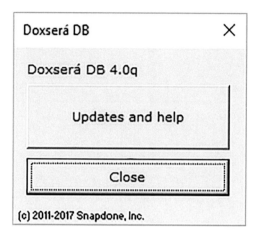

Clicking on the About Command displays an information box showing the version of the Program you currently have installed. If you want to see if there have been any updates, click on the Update and Help button.

Updates

If you click on the Update and Help button and determine that you need to update the version of the Program you have, follow the instructions on "Update" on page 109.

Options

When you click on the Options Command you will see a menu showing these subcommands: **Authoring** (this subcommand does NOT appear in TheFormTool PRO), **Holidays, License Code, License Agreement, Manage License** (this subcommand does NOT appear in TheFormTool PRO), **Metadata Scrubbing, Path, Outlook** (this subcommand does NOT appear in TheFormTool PRO or in Doxserá), and **Uninstall**.

This section explains the subcommands under this Command.

Authoring

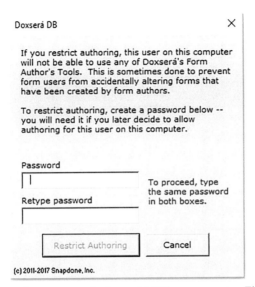

This subcommand does NOT appear in TheForm-Tool PRO. This subcommand may be used to require the entry of a password to make any Form Authoring changes to the Template.

NOTE WELL: This subcommand applies to ALL FORMS under this license, not just the Form you are currently using.

If you have people using the Template whom you do not want to be able to change the Template, click on this subcommand and enter the password you want to use and click on the Restrict Authoring button. This will prevent anyone from changing the Template.

If you later want someone to make changes to the Template, click on the Authoring subcommand again, enter the password, and click on the Unlock Authoring button.

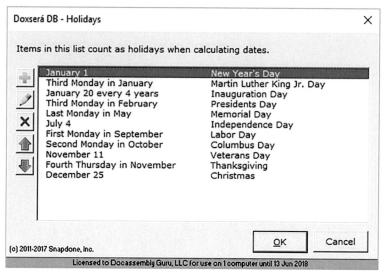

This is an automatic list of eleven official US holidays, but you can edit this list as you desire. This list is used **only** if the Form Author has created date offsets in preparing the Template and so it may or may not be applicable to your Templates. If you are unsure about this, ask your Form Author.

A date offset is where one date in the Template is dependent upon a date given as an Answer. For example, you may be asked to enter a date for some reason and the Template will also automatically put in some other date, like the first of the next month, dependent upon the date you enter and upon the date offset used by the Form Author.

If the Answers in your Template request dates, you should probably review and possibly edit the Holidays.

To add a Holiday

- Click on the Holiday subcommand.

- Click on the Green Plus symbol to the left of the dialog box.

- Enter the name of the Holiday in the appropriate area.

- The Holiday will either fall on a specific date, or it will be determined by a relationship (offset) to another date.

- If it falls on a specific date, enter that date using the drop-down lists beside month, day, and year. For year, you can either choose "every year" or select a specific year.

- If it is dependent on another date, click on the button beside "Offset from January 1" and use the drop-down lists to determine the date you want. The formula for determining the date you want is shown in the box. If computing your Holiday is complex, you may want to get the assistance of your Form Author.

If you want to edit a given Holiday, click on the name of the Holiday and then click on the edit button (pencil symbol). Then complete the dialog box in a manner similar to that given above for adding a Holiday.

If you want to delete a Holiday, simply click on the name of the Holiday and click on the Red "X" to the left of the list of Holidays.

License Code

This subcommand allows you to enter the registered name in which the Program is licensed and the license code. If you need to enter this information, you can always get it from the Program website if you have forgotten it.

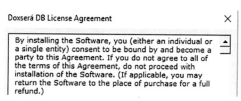

Since this information must be entered exactly as it is on the Program website, it is usually best to copy and paste from the website.

License Agreement

Doxserá DB License Agreement ✕

By installing the Software, you (either an individual or a single entity) consent to be bound by and become a party to this Agreement. If you do not agree to all of the terms of this Agreement, do not proceed with installation of the Software. (If applicable, you may return the Software to the place of purchase for a full refund.)

The License Agreement subcommand will show you the legal license agreement you agreed to in using the Program.

Manage license

This subcommand does NOT appear in TheForm-Tool PRO. While you may load the Program on more than one computer, a Program license is only good for one specific computer at a time.

If you want to use the Program on a computer, but another computer is already licensed to use the Program, click on this subcommand.

This will show you the computers which contain this license, and you can remove the computer you are not using. When you go back to the original computer, you will have to go through this process again to remove the other computer.

This subcommand can also apply to people instead of computers if you click in the "people" space. The choice is up to you.

Metadata Scrubbing

Word automatically adds a lot of hidden information about each Document. This hidden information is called metadata.

If you want to have all the metadata in a Document scrubbed completely and invisibily when you Petrify the Form, click on this subcommand. When you do turn on Metadata Scrubbing, it will affect ALL Forms which you Petrify.

This subcommand can toggle between being turned on and being turned off, so if you change your mind, simply click on the subcommand again and follow directions.

Outlook

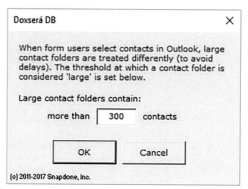

This subcommand does NOT appear in The**Form**Tool PRO or in **Dox**será. This subcommand controls the method used when Outlook files are used in the Template. If Outlook files are used in your Template, contact your Form Author to determine how this subcommand should be use.

Path

Program information, such as saved Answers, saved Questionnaires, Holidays, Master Lists, Folios, and Wrappers is maintained in Folders originally on the local computer. If you want to move that information to the Cloud or to a server, you need to change the Path to that different shared location.

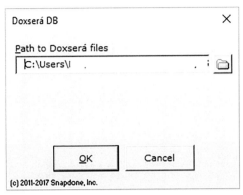

If you have previously saved information on the local computer and you want to change the Path, you will be asked if you want to copy that information to the shared location, which is usually but not always a good idea.

If you are using multiple computers, be sure the Path for each computer is set to the same shared location.

Uninstall

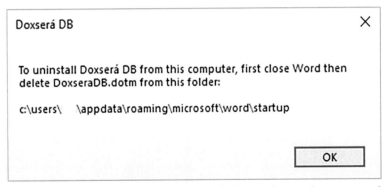

To uninstall the Program, click on this subcommand and follow the instructions.

Templates

Templates vs. docx

A description of Templates and Word Documents is on "The Different Forms You Will Be Using" on page 7.

It is important that you have the end-users open Templates when they are working on a new Form. The problem, of course, is that if they open a Form and work on it, when they are through they will most likely save the Document. When they do that, they have just overwritten the file they opened.

By opening the Form using a Template, the Template itself will remain unchanged. The Form which then opens is a new Form and when they save it, they will be required to name the Folder and filename it is to be saved as.

Filing Templates

Templates may be saved wherever you want on the computer or server as long as you let Word know the location of the folder and allow that Folder to show when the end-user is locating Templates.

The particular hierarchy you use will be one you need to set up. My only recommendation is that you are consistent in the naming of the Folders and subfolders to make it easy for the end-user to locate the Templates. For example, if a law firm were setting up the Template Folders and subfolders, they may have different Folders for litigation, estate planning, and real estate. Then, within each of those folders, they might have subfolders for the various court documents, wills, trusts, required real estate forms, optional real estate forms, etc.

To set up the folders and let Word know the location of the folder(s), follow your Word instructions for the version of Word you have.

Maintenance

Update

From time-to-time TheFormTool, LLC updates the various Programs. Although they may notify you by email of these updates, some updates may be made to the Programs without notification to you.

I suggest that at least once a week you click on the About Command (see "About" on page 98). Then notice the version of the Program you have.

1. Next, click on the **Updates and Help** button. This will take you to the website which will show you the most recent version of the Program.

2. If the Program has been updated, simply click on the **Download Now!** button on the website.

This will cause a .zip file to be downloaded to your computer.

3. Then <u>be sure Word is closed</u>.

4. Next extract the .zip files as explained in "How To Install the Program" on page 81.

5. Next click on the .docm file for your Program and follow the instructions given.

When the Program has been installed, close Word and reopen it. The updated Program will now be on this computer.

Be sure you update all your computers to the same version if you have the Program installed on more than one computer.

Uninstall

When you update the Program, you do not need to uninstall it. However, there may be times when you want to uninstall it. To do this, click on the Options Command and then on the Uninstall Command as explained on "Uninstall" on page 105. Then follow the directions given in the instruction box.

Glossary

Add	A Command which will add an Answer space for a Serial Answer or a row for a Grid.
Administrator	The person who will install the Program and maintain the Program.
Answer	The information supplied by the End-User in response to a Question.
Attention Marker	A Dialog Box which appears after the End-User has "Filled" the Form. This Dialog Box contains information to which the attention of the End-User is directed to enter additional information or to be sure something in the Form is correct.

Attn	A Command which allows the End-User to go to the next Attention Marker.
Blanks	A Command which inserts blank spaces in the Form wherever the Form Author has provided for an Variable to be shown.
Boilerplate	Those portions of a Template, Form, or Document which remain constant in every situation.
Category	A "folder" used to contain Form Sets which are similar to each other. Categories are arranged in a hierarchical structure similar to the Windows folder structure.
Checklist	An Answer which contains multiple possibilities, any or all of which may be selected.
Clear Answers	A Command which clears all of the Answers which have been entered in the Questionnaire and in any Grids.
Commands	Items in the Program Tab which, when clicked on by the End-User, cause the Program to do something.
Default	An Answer which has been provided by the Form Author as the most likely Answer. It may be accepted or changed by the End-User.
Derived	An Answer which is a formula or calculation provided by the Form Author. It is not to be changed except by the Form Author.

Dialog Box	A Windows box which allows the user to provide detailed information to be used by the Program.
Document	A Word Document which can be altered by the user and then saved, deleted, or printed as the user decides.
Document Assembly	The process of using a Program which permits the entry of Variables and then assembles a Document using those Variables and other Program logic provided by the Form Author.
Document Automation	Another term for Document Assembly.
Down	A Command which moves the selected Series Answer or Grid row down one Answer space or one row.
Drop-down	An Answer which contains multiple possibilities, of which only one may be chosen.
End-User	The day-to-day user of the Program as well as of the Templates and Forms provided by a Form Author.
Expert Guide	The excellent and detailed manual provided by TheFormTool, LLC explaining the Program and how to use it. The Expert Guide is provided free to anyone who has the Program.
Fetch	A Command in **Dox**será or **Dox**será **DB** to select Answers from a Folio or Data Source.

Fill	A Command which completes the logic of the Form and inputs the correct information in the appropriate places to produce an "error-free" Document.
Folio	A "hidden" document containing a library of text clauses or paragraphs, graphics, footnotes, and other non-text features which may be used in **Dox**será or **Dox**será **DB**. The Questionnaire may allow the End-User to select which of the items in the Folio are to be used in the Form.
Form	A Word Document which contains a Program Questionnaire and possibly one or more Grids, and which has been created by a Form Author to use the Answers to create a finished Document.
Form Author	The person who has created a Template or Form using the Program and its logic.
Form Set	A combination of different Forms for which the Program creates a single Questionnaire so each Question is only Answered once. When the Question-naire is completed, the Program will produce all the Documents created by the Forms in the particular Form Set.
Format	An instructional template showing the way an Answer is to be entered, e.g., "Enter the date as mm/dd/yyyy" which means the Answer is to be entered similar to 10/02/2017.

Grid	A Series Answer form which is always separate from and below the Question-naire. A Grid appears as a spreadsheet containing rows and columns. The Question for each cell is contained in the header for that column. There may be more than one Grid in a Form.
Group	A section of the Program Tab which contains several related Commands.
Information Box	A Windows box which contains information for the End-User but does not provide for the entry of information.
Linked	A Series Answer which is dependent on and linked to a Linking Answer. If the Linking Answer changes, the End-User must appropriately change the Linked Answer. If a Linked Answer is in the Questionnaire it will appear as [??]:[??]. A Linked Answer in a Grid will be each of the Answers in every column except those in the left-most column.
Linking	A Series Answer which is a controlling Answer for any Linked Answer. The information in a Linking Answer is to be completed before a Linked Answer is completed. If a Linking Answer appears in the Questionnaire it will appear as more than one [??] stacked on top of each other. The Answers in the left-most column of a Grid are always Linking Answers.

Peek Next	A Command which allows the End-User to see the next location of an Answer in the Form.
Peek Off	A Command which turns off the Peek Next Command and removes the split-screen.
Petrify	A Command which removes the Questionnaire and any Grids from the "Filled" Document and permanently sets the Answers in the finished Document.
Program	Either The**FormTool** PRO, **Doxserá**, or **Doxserá DB** which is used by the End-User or the Administrator.
Program Tab	The Tab in the Ribbon which is added when the Program is installed and which provides the Commands for the Program.
Question	An interrogatory in a Questionnaire or a Grid to which the End-User provides an Answer.
Questionnaire	A table of Questions and Answers which provides a space for the End-User to enter information which will be used by the Program to complete the Form. There can be only one Questionnaire for each Form. The Questionnaire is always at the end of the Form but above any Grids.
Refresh	A Command which provides the connections between Linking and Linked Answers in the Questionnaire.

Remove	A Command which deletes a Serial Answer in a Questionnaire or a row in a Grid.
Reset	A Command which refreshes all the Variables in a Form back to their original state, including those in a Derived Answer.
Ribbon	The Word row of Tabs and Commands which is usually at the top of each Word screen.
Save/Load	A Command which allows the End-User to either save the Answers for re-use in the same or another Form, or load Answers which have been previously saved into a Questionnaire.
Series	An Answer which may contain multiple separate items of information in response to a Question.
Start	A Command which moves the cursor to the first Answer in a Questionnaire when a Form is open. In **Dox**será and **Dox**será **DB**, if no Document or Form is open, this Command opens the Form Set Dialog Box.
Template	A Form which has been created by a Form Author but which is saved in the Word template (.dotx or .dotm) format. Upon opening the Template, Word copies the information in the Template into a separate Form. Saving, changing, or deleting this separate Form does not affect the Template in any way.

Text	An Answer which may contain any information which is input by the End-User. A Text Answer may be text, numerical, or date information.
Tools	A Command which opens a list of subcommands which can be used by the End-User or Administrator.
Up	A Command which moves the selected Series Answer or Grid row up one Answer space or one row.
Variable	Any item in a Template, Form, or Document which can be changed depending on the situation.
Word	The Microsoft Word program.
Yes/no	An Answer which contains only Yes or No in response to the Question. If the Form Author has provided, it may also contain n/a which stands for Not Applicable. The End-User may select only one Answer.

Index

N

network 82, 83
Normal. *See* Commands: Fetch

O

Options. *See* Commands
Outlook. *See* Commands

P

Path. *See* Commands
PDF 64, 71
Peek Next. *See* Commands
Peek Off. *See* Commands
Petrification 62, 63, 70
Petrified 10
Prepare to Share. *See* Commands
Program i, ii, iii, iv, v, 2, 3, 4, 7, 9, 10, 13, 16, 19, 20, 23, 24, 25, 26, 29,
    30, 31, 32, 34, 36, 37, 44, 46, 49, 50, 51, 54, 56, 62, 63, 64, 65, 68,
    71, 72, 77, 78, 81, 82, 85, 87, 88, 91, 92, 94, 95, 97, 98, 101, 102,
    104, 105, 109, 110, 111, 112, 113, 114, 115, 116
Program Tab 2, 13, 19, 23, 24, 26, 29, 30, 36, 44, 46, 51, 54, 68, 85

Q

Question 2, 14, 15, 16, 17, 19, 21, 22, 23, 26, 36, 54, 56, 68, 86, 111, 114,
    115, 116, 117, 118
Questionnaire 2, 11, 13, 14, 15, 20, 21, 22, 24, 25, 31, 32, 34, 35, 36, 37,
    41, 42, 43, 44, 46, 47, 50, 51, 55, 56, 62, 63, 67, 68, 71, 78, 86, 87,
    88, 92, 93, 94, 95, 96, 112, 114, 115, 116, 117

R

Red "X" 39, 58, 60, 61, 101
Refresh. *See* Commands
Registration Name 83
Remove. *See* Commands
Remove Content 95
Reset. *See* Commands
Restrict Authoring 99
Row/Column. *See* Commands

S

Save and Close 89, 90
Save/Load. *See* Commands

Made in the USA
San Bernardino, CA
15 February 2018